How to be Evangelistic without being Religious

Graham Horsley

HEADLINE SPECIAL

Published for **Headway** by

MOORLEY'S Print & Publishing

British Library Cataloguing in Publication Data.
A catalogue record for this book is available from the British Library.

ISBN 086071 588 4

MOORLEY'S Print & Publishing
23 Park Rd., Ilkeston, Derbys DE7 5DA
Tel/Fax: (0115) 932 0643

The harvest is plentiful?

He told them, "The harvest is plentiful, but the workers are few. Ask the Lord of the harvest, therefore, to send out workers into his harvest field."

Luke 10:2 (New International Version)

These words of Jesus prepare the disciples for their first experience of being sent out as evangelists (literally people with good news to share). Their experience proves him to be correct.

The seventy-two returned with joy and said, "Lord, even the demons submit to us in your name."

Luke 10:17

However, many Christians doubt that this is still true. As I travel round the country I often hear phrases like:

"This place is very hard spiritually." (I've lost count of the places that describe themselves as the 'hardest place in Britain to evangelise'!)

"People aren't interested in Church/Christianity anymore."

"We've visited the whole area, but no-one's interested."

I believe that the words of Jesus are as true today as they were when he spoke them. They hold good in every time and place because all people are created in the image of God and are therefore spiritual beings. Every one of us has a yearning for spiritual reality that will never be satisfied until we are in a right relationship with God our Father and receive spiritual nourishment from him. This is only possible through faith in Jesus Christ, his life, death and resurrection.

Paradoxically I believe that the experience of many British Christians described above is also true. They have worked hard and been faithful but have seen very little reward for their efforts and their faithfulness. How can this be? Let us examine both statements and see how they can both be true even though they appear at first sight to be contradictory.

The harvest is plentiful

Many people have observed an increasing interest in the spiritual. This is demonstrated in many ways:

- 72% of the population declared themselves 'Christian' in the 2001 census. This may be a statement about culture and heritage rather than belief, but it is still a significant statistic.
- In 2000 35% of babies born were brought to Anglican, Methodist, Presbyterian or Roman Catholic Churches for baptism. How do we explain this spiritual longing on the part of parents who for the most part have little connection with Church themselves?
- In 1987, 48% of the population reported having religious or spiritual experiences; by 2000, this had increased to 76% of the population. David Hay, who conducted the 1987 survey concludes that the increase in reported experiences was not because there are now more experiences, but that the climate has changed and people are more willing to admit to having such experiences now.
- The second most frequently visited web-sites today (after porn) are those concerned with the mystical and spiritual.
- The Assessment and Qualifications Alliance (AQA), the biggest of the three exam boards, reports a 21% increase from 2000 to 2004 in the choice of Religious Studies at A level. Philosophy has increased by 67% in the same period.[1]

[1] Evangelism in a Spiritual Age, Steven Croft et al, Church House Publishing, 2005, pp9-10

- Some business gurus have commented that society in America although still a consumer society is undergoing a subtle shift from being consumers of things (material possessions) to becoming consumers of experiences. This explains, for instance, the huge growth in extreme sports, but also the increase in seeking spiritual experiences of all kinds.[2]

A hard place to harvest?

At first glance this appears to be good news for the Christian Church. The picture is, however, not that simple. The Church and Christianity are not perceived by those outside it as 'spiritual' – they are 'religious' which is not good. A recent survey which looked at the attitudes to faith and church by interviewing people chosen specifically because they were completely outside the church found:

Christianity was synonymous with 'Church' and the Church was tarred with the brush of religion, a word with so many negative connotations that it was used almost as an insult.[3]

People, many of whom had little recent experience, considered it (church) embarrassing, dull, narrow, bigoted, hypocritical, unfriendly, unreal, prescriptive, judgmental, patriarchal, unquestioning, inflexible, nerve-wracking, alienating, corrupt and unable to handle doubt.[4]

It comes as a shock for many Christians that people outside the church (and the other faith traditions) consider themselves more spiritual than Christians, but this is the case. If our approach to evangelism makes the assumption that we as Christians are bringing spiritual values to people who don't have any, we are in for a rude awakening.

---

2 The Experience Economy, B Joseph Pine & James Gilmore, Harvard Business School Press 1999

3 Evangelism in a Spiritual Age, Steven Croft et al, Church House Publishing 2005, p41

4 ibid p48

The media have reported spiritual issues in more depth in recent years, however, their coverage of Church and institutional Christianity is often negative. For instance, the media coverage of the impact of the life of the recently deceased Pope John Paul II concentrated to a large extent on the Pope's maintenance of a traditional view of human sexuality (homophobic!) and particularly the impact of his negativity towards condoms and its effect on the rise of HIV/aids in Africa. This is the back-drop which shapes the attitudes and prejudices of many outside the church. This despite the fact that many people actually have positive experiences of church:

... there were numerous positive experiences of church, from respondents of all ages and backgrounds. Those positive experiences spoke of church that were welcoming, connected to real life, lively and energetic and offered a sense of worth and belonging. They were places that offered a sense of 'love', 'understanding', 'support', 'peace' and were about 'communicat[ing]' and 'shar[ing]'.[5]

These experiences are seen as unusual and do not significantly challenge deeply held prejudices about Church in general.

A further problem for the church is that religion is seen as intolerant. Strangely it seems that a 'tolerant' society is extremely intolerant towards people who hold to different values.

Tolerance was the unquestioned supreme deity in the respondents' universe of values. Intolerance was the greatest sin. Those social groups deemed to disagree with this were not tolerated. Tolerance was, however, in the eye of the beholder,

---

5 ibid p49

with each individual drawing the boundary, with intolerance on one side and 'political correctness' on the other.[6]

Firstly, it was quite clear that it was ***my*** *definition of tolerance which was right. Other definitions were wrong, being either too tight ('intolerant') or too broad ('politically correct').*[7]

A further problem for the Church and especially the Methodist Church is that there is in many (though not all) churches a chronic lack of confidence about engagement in evangelism. A survey in 2001 found that only 7% of Methodists were involved in evangelism (13% for all Christians), whereas 23% of Methodists were involved in community service (15% for all Christians).[8] Methodist DNA is very much about demonstrating the love of Christ in practical ways, but not being confident about explaining the source of that love or encouraging others to receive that love for themselves. A somewhat cynical definition of the Methodist approach to holistic mission might be:

Love people until they ask why and then fudge it!

There are a number of reasons for this:

- We (rightly) discern that many people believe that faith is personal and is not meant to be shared.
- We have rejected some traditional approaches to evangelism as being ineffective, but haven't yet discovered new approaches that might be effective.
- We instinctively recognise that the church that meets our spiritual needs well may not meet the spiritual needs of our friends/family/workmates.

---

6 Beyond Belief, Nick Spenser, LICC, 2003 p20

7 ibid p21

8 Church Life Profile 2001: Denominational Results for Methodist Church, Phillip Escott & Alison Gelder, CIM, 2002, p25

- We are not sure that the faith that helps us to make sense of our lives will be helpful to others.
- We have a longing to share our faith, but are unsure how to go about it.

The factors outlined above lead us to a situation where the Church often feels powerless and inadequate to respond to the spiritual needs of the people around us. The world has changed in a way that leaves us feeling out of touch and ill-prepared for effective mission. In these circumstances there are a number of reactions that are not helpful:

- Develop a siege mentality. No-one is interested in Church anymore, so we will become a club of like-minded people who cling together for security in a hostile world with which we do not engage at a faith level.
- Develop a blame culture. It's someone else's fault – we need a new minister, steward, organist, circuit leadership, national leadership etc.
- Develop a guilt culture. We know that old-fashioned evangelistic approaches are not bearing fruit, so we work harder, become more strident and yet despite all our efforts, we only attract an audience of Christians who have been converted years ago.
- Condemn those who are not interested in church as unspiritual, hard-hearted and sinful.

If these approaches are not helpful, how can we find a way forward?

I propose to answer that question in three ways:

1. We need to understand some of the important ways that society has changed in a way that impacts our evangelism
2. We need to explore a Biblical methodology for evangelism

3. We need to identify some practical things that Christians and local churches can do to build confidence.

A changing world

In a lecture at Cliff College, George Hunter commented that if next year were 1955, the American Methodist Church was perfectly poised to make the most of its evangelistic opportunities. He went on to say that the British Methodist Church is about 50 years behind the American. For many Christians today there is a profound sense of wishing we could return to a safer age where there were a lot more certainties about the relationship between Church and society. This is partly a longing for an age that never was, and is partly a recognition that the world has changed dramatically and is continuing to change at an ever increasing pace – change is here to stay!

Our challenge is to learn to engage evangelistically with society as it is rather than as we would like it to be. We live in a world dominated by consumer choice and people are less willing than they have ever been to 'put up' with a church which does not meet their needs. They vote with their feet. This has led to an increasing diversity in styles of church (and particularly of worship). Whether you think this is good or bad is irrelevant – it's a fact of life that every church has to take seriously.

It is also true that the way that people understand their religious longings has changed dramatically in the last two or three decades and the Church has not always kept pace with these changes.

What are these changes?

- From being religious to being spiritual
- From organisation to organism
- From joining to joining in

- From living in a single community to living in a multitude of networks
- From seeking explanations to seeking experiences
- From truth to truths
- From Christendom to post-Christendom

1. From being religious to being spiritual

We have already referred to this in the introduction. The fact that people are more open to the spiritual is not all good news. Much of what passes for spirituality is actually consumerism – I want spiritual experiences that make me feel good. A truly Christian spiritual experience may make us feel good, more importantly it will challenge us to live counter-cultural lives. If we are disciples of Jesus we must take up our cross daily and live as he would have us live. This is a big challenge for those within the church never mind those outside it. A spirituality that 'pick and mixes' from all sort of sources is eventually going to be confronted with some hard choices in the Christian faith. However, if we do not engage people at this 'spiritual' level, they will not engage with Christianity at all.

2. From organisation to organism

In the past, the Church has relied quite heavily on its status as the 'religious institution' to engage with its community. Though some ministers may refer disparagingly to the 'hatch, match and dispatch' approach to religion, it has provided a lot of fertile encounters with people from outside the church (though they would not necessarily see themselves that way). As less people come to the Church for rites of passage or perceive the church as the place where their lives are given religious meaning, the church is faced with the challenge of doing evangelism via individual relationships rather than through its institutional presence. The new churches have had to learn this lesson already and they have much to teach us in this area.

3. From joining to joining in

This is another symptom of the rejection of institutions. Christians often expect that the fact that someone has a profound religious experience will automatically lead to their full involvement in the life of the local church. They are dismayed when this does not happen. For those outside the church a good experience does not naturally lead to committed membership of the group which helped them to enjoy that experience. They see it more like enjoying a concert in a particular venue – their enjoyment does not mean that they will then attend every event at that venue. A church which places a high value on faithfulness and duty finds it hard to cope with people who naturally exercise choice. This is illustrated beautifully by a quote from a lady who could not understand why the Church should impose conditions before agreeing to marry her and her fiancée:

The Church should reflect what we want. The Church should not dictate to us that you can get married, you can't get married. We want to get married. We are consumers of the Church.[9]

4. From living in a single community to living in a multitude of networks

Despite John Wesley's assertion that 'the world is my parish', most Methodist churches instinctively expect that they will serve the geographic community immediately surrounding their building. This approach was formed in an age where social mobility was much lower and where people lived, worked, played and shared in the life of the extended family in the same fairly small geographic area. Many people today live in a number of different networks: they live (or should that be sleep!) in one place, they work in another, they go somewhere else for leisure activities and their extended families are spread all over the country. This is further complicated by the break down of the nuclear family so that one can no longer assume

---

9 Beyond Belief, Nick Spencer, LICC p26

that mum, dad and 2.4 children live at the same address. The reality for many people is a series of relationships with children sharing in the life of different families at different stages of their lives (or even their weeks). Where does church fit in this complex set of networks? For many it's another network which has little congruence with their other networks – no wonder that it's so hard to develop a meaningful pattern of discipleship. It was much simpler when the people you worshipped with on Sunday were the people you worked with on Monday to Friday and played with on Saturday, and where whole families belonged to the same church. Mutual support and encouragement was easily delivered – now we need quite sophisticated mechanisms and relationships to achieve the same quality of support.

5. From seeking explanations to seeking experiences

Throughout the modern era, the Church has worked hard at making intellectual sense. It has wrestled with the challenges of science and philosophy. Apologetics have been given a high priority in the evangelistic approach of the church. The problem is that we are often offering very sophisticated answers to questions that no-one is asking! There is a proper place for apologetics, but it comes much later in an evangelistic encounter than many people expect. A visit to a 'body, mind and spirit' fair will quickly show that people are willing to pay generously for all sorts of spiritual experiences which have the most sketchy scientific or philosophical explanation. Experience is in! If we are to engage in apologetics, then our apologetic task is to explain people's experiences and encounters with God (or the 'supernatural'). Our first task then is to help people to have such experiences and then recognise that a relationship with Jesus Christ, both enhances and explains these experiences. This has profound implications for the way we do evangelism and worship. Much Methodist worship is wordy and cerebral. We do not always expect or encourage people to encounter God in life-changing ways. In 'Europe: the exceptional case', Grace Davie comments[10] that in the places where the Christian Church is growing. Pentecostalism is a strong feature with its concentration on the power of the Holy Spirit, healing miracles and exorcisms – this is one (but not the only) way of emphasising the importance of experience. One of the common features of growing churches and effective evangelists is an expectation that God will intervene in life-changing ways, and a willingness to take all sorts of experiences seriously. If it is true that 76% of the population have had life-changing supernatural experiences, dare we approach our encounters with people outside the church with the expectation that God is already at work in their lives in ways that they are seeking to understand. Even if the language they use to describe these experiences is very different from our 'churchy' way of talking about such things.

6. From truth to truths

This an area where evangelical Christians often have great difficulty. A much beloved quotation of evangelists is the words of Jesus in John 8:32: *"Then you will know the truth, and the truth will set you free."*

It is undoubtedly true that there is one overarching truth which is revealed in Jesus Christ. I do not want to deny this or imply in any way that this has changed. However, what has changed is that most people do not perceive things this way. The Manic Street Preachers (a rock band – not an evangelism agency!) issued a CD in 1998 entitled "This is my truth, tell me yours". Whatever you think of the music, this encapsulates how most people today think of truth. There isn't one truth – there is my truth. My truth works for me in providing a framework of meaning for my life. There's no reason whatsoever that it should work for you – though I'm happy to share it with you if you're interested. An evangelistic approach that implies that the evangelist knows the truth and his hearer does not

10 Europe: the exceptional case, Grace Davie, Darton, Longman & Todd, 2002

(sometimes called the 'jug to mug' approach) is unlikely to be well received. An approach that begins by sharing my experience of what makes sense of my life is much more likely to receive a sympathetic listening. If adopting this approach then the "tell me yours" part of the Manic Street Preachers album title is also important – sharing is a two way process. This implies a testimony based approach to evangelism – I share the story of what God has done in my life and trust that my hearer has the wit to ask the question – 'would this work for me too?' This approach has strong resonance with the approach of Jesus in sharing with the spiritual seekers that he met. As Christians, we believe that 'my truth' definitely is a 'universal truth', but we do not preach this, we wait for our hearers to work it out for themselves. As I listen to another person's version of 'my truth', I do not look to see where they are wrong in order to correct them, I look for signs of the Holy Spirit at work to encourage them.

7. From Christendom to post-Christendom

At its simplest, this means that there is no longer a Christian framework underpinning the whole of society. Law, morality and values are no longer shaped by Christian values. It also has a profound impact on the way the Church understands its ministry. If we live in a Christian world where every household has a local church to which it belongs (however nominally), then the primary duty of the Church is pastoral care, Christian education and sacramental worship. If we live in a post-Christendom world, then the primary calling of the church is to mission. Mission to culture and society in the widest sense, mission to individuals in terms of a practical demonstration of the love of Christ and mission in the sense of calling and challenging people to turn away from a life in rebellion to God and to turn to Christ as Lord and Saviour.

These changes in societal values and the continuing drift of Christians away from church has led to a society which can be characterised as below:[11]

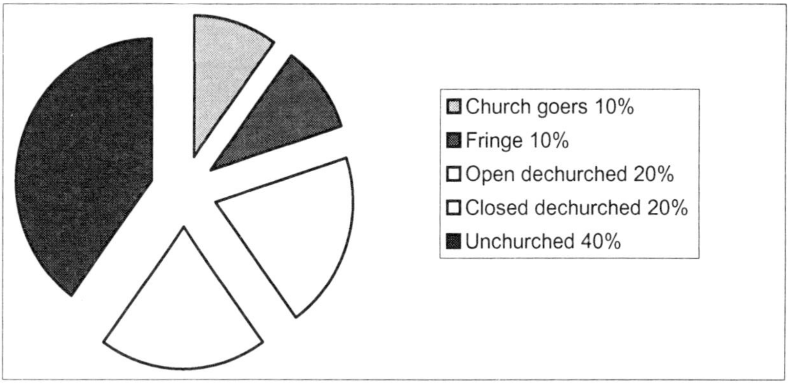

10% regular churchgoers – the evangelists?

10% fringe – these are the people who have meaningful contacts with a local church and attend occasionally. When I began as a Methodist minister 25 years ago, evangelism was normally understood as putting on an event in Church and persuading the fringe to attend in the hope that they would become fully committed followers of Jesus and members of the Church. This is still a valid method of evangelism, but the number of people who we can hope to reach in this way is quite small (for the church, as for me and a number of other 50-something men, the fringe isn't what it used to be!).

40% dechurched – these are the people who used to go to church but are no longer involved. They are divided equally into:

20% open dechurched – these are people who no longer attend church but still have affectionate memories of church.

11 Mission Shaped Church, Graham Cray et al, Church House Publishing 2004 pp36-37

Life got busy and without ever meaning to, they drifted away from church. They will almost certainly want to get married in church and have their children christened. However, once you have stopped attending church, it is difficult to go back. The church planting movement in the 1990's was remarkably effective at re-churching the dechurched. The less formal, more contemporary fresh approach of the new congregations was very attractive to the de-churched. It was still recognisably church, but more lively! Their newness also made it possible for people to return without feeling guilty for having been away for so long.

20% closed dechurched – these are the people who have left church and have no intention of ever going back. They are the most resistant group to evangelism. Some left church because of personality issues - they had an argument with the minister or the members. Others have undergone a crisis of faith and have rejected all that church stands for. Others have felt (rightly or wrongly) that they were excluded by the church – often because of behavioural or moral issues. Whatever the reason why these people left, the only possible way to win them back is to go in a spirit of repentance and say that we are sorry that their experience of Church left them hurt and angry.

40% unchurched – these are the people who have never had any meaningful contact with church. They are not particularly anti-church – church is irrelevant to their lives. All they know of the church is second-hand. The only way to make any contact with them is by personal relationships. Evangelising this group is no different to the process involved in becoming an overseas missionary. We need to understand their culture and work out how to communicate faith and to be church in appropriate ways. As long as we expect these people to take on 'chapel culture' in order to become Christians, we will only see minimal evangelistic impact.

These proportions give cause for both concern and hope. 30% of the population (fringe plus open dechurched) are open to an invitation to become members of church as we know it. This gives considerable scope for evangelism. The bad news is that 60% of the population is resistant to this approach to evangelism. They will require a different approach and almost certainly a different shape of church (and even the word church is unhelpful in this context) in order to become disciples of Jesus Christ.

However, these figures are extremely age sensitive. Most of the fringe and the open dechurched are at the older end of the spectrum, the completely unchurched dominate the younger end of the spectrum. Churches which are struggling to retain the children (and grandchildren) of their committed members are ill-equipped to evangelise those outside the church. It is particularly in the 20s-30s age group that fresh expressions of church are vital. If we are not willing to concentrate our remaining resources in this area in ways which will risk completely new way of working – the future of the church is bleak. To achieve this, it is vital that circuits see themselves as large mission units rather than administration units of smaller churches. Most circuits have the resources to facilitate at least one fresh expression of church. If they are willing to put quality resources into this rather than relying on busy leaders doing this in addition to a traditional pastoral load, then there is every chance of success. There are encouraging signs that increasing numbers of circuits are doing this, though it's too early to be able to see what the results will be.[12] The recently adopted priorities of the Methodist Church about encouraging Fresh Ways of Being Church demonstrate a clear desire that this should happen and the appointment of Revd Peter Pillinger (from September 2005) as a Methodist team member to the Fresh Expressions mission agency is also a hopeful sign.

---

12 see www.freshexpressions.org.uk for a register of these in the Methodist, Anglican and some other denominations.

A Biblical methodology of evangelism

Underlying Assumptions

1. There is an assumption in all the New Testament literature that all people will benefit from accepting Jesus Christ as their Lord, whatever their faith (the New Testament doesn't entertain the possibility of no faith!). There are therefore, no no-go areas for evangelism. This is not the same as saying there are no unacceptable forms of evangelism!
2. The Methodist doctrine of prevenient grace reminds us that God is at work in all sorts of ways. To assume that every religious experience outside orthodox Christianity is counterfeit denies this doctrine. One of the hardest tasks of the evangelist is continually searching for signs of the Holy Spirit at work in the strangest places and most unexpected people and joining in appropriately.
3. Our practice of evangelism continually challenges our understanding of Church. If evangelism is 'initiation into the Kingdom of God'[13], and one of the visible signs of that initiation is joining a community of Christians, then the appropriateness of the Christian community for those who are seeking faith and being nurtured in the early stages of faith is crucial. Sometimes we unwittingly reject the linkage of faith-sharing and church membership because we intuitively realise that our particular Christian community is inappropriate to their spiritual development, but do not go far enough and ask the question, "What Christian community will help these people to truly enter into the Kingdom of God?"

---

13 William Abraham's definition in 'The Logic of Evangelism'

A helpful model of evangelism?

Andrew Jones[14] has developed a model of evangelism based on the sending of the seventy-two in Luke 10. He analyses the principal verbs in the passage to shape his model:

- Go (v3)
- Enter (v5)
- Stay (v7)
- Eat & Drink (v7)
- Heal (v9)
- Tell (v9)

Go! Mission is not concerned with attracting people to us, but going out to meet with them. Many churches base their evangelistic strategy on a 'come' rather than a 'go' model. Fortunately we do not have to go far to encounter spiritually minded people who are outside the church.

Enter the homes and lives of those who are receptive. In the New Testament they were often the 'God-fearers' in the synagogues of the diaspora. They were the first to respond positively to the Good News of Jesus. Who are these people today? They are probably the spiritual seekers, some of whom belong to the great world religions and some of whom are spiritual without being religious in the orthodox sense. We can only enter where we are made welcome, so who in your area or network is willing to welcome you into their lives?

Stay – sharing is a long process that involves entering into another culture and staying long enough to understand it. Listening for a long time before speaking. Understanding the unspoken values and discerning the spiritual framework underlying them.

---

14 Otherwise known as the 'tallskinnykiwi' – unpublished see http://tallskinnykiwi.typepad.com

Eat & Drink – hospitality has elements of welcome and acceptance. There is an implicit acceptance of other people's way of living and not an imposition of one's own culture. Perhaps one of the tests of whether we have stayed long enough in a culture is whether we are perceived as guests or as family when we eat and drink with people. One of the reasons for the undoubted success of the Alpha Course is the very different atmosphere which is created when a group share a meal before beginning to talk about faith.

Heal – two elements interweave in this one theme: compassion and the power of God. Compassion is a longing for the person in whose life we are sharing to be whole. Healing involves body, mind and spirit. Praying for someone's healing often involves becoming part of the answer to one's own prayer. It is also about expecting that the Holy Spirit will meet people's felt needs in a way that will make them look to God in a new way. It's important that both elements are present. Compassion without power is noble but not particularly helpful. Power without compassion is arrogant. When the two come together, people often (though not always) begin to ask the 'why' questions that naturally lead into faith-sharing.

Tell – this is the last element in the progression – not the first as many evangelistic programmes suggest. Telling is in a cultural context that the evangelist has taken time to understand. It is also worth noting that the Jesus way of telling is usually more provocative than proclamatory. He spoke in parables which were largely unexplained and capable of more than one interpretation. Explanations were for those who took time to seek them out and ask detailed questions. Jesus was unafraid to let people walk away and was happy to work with the small number who sought him out. Even then, Jesus' normal way of answering questions was to ask another question that assumed real spiritual significance in the first question.

A 21st Century approach to evangelism will take on these sort of characteristics. Faith-sharing will always seek to provoke questions by loving actions and experiences of the power of God. Many people today are curious about religious experience, but totally unmoved by Christian doctrine. The beginnings of 'telling' will normally be the sharing of my experience of the love of Christ and the difference it has made to my life. We do not need to tell people that they can have the same experience – they can work that out for themselves and will either choose to talk to us about it or to walk away. Even those who walk away often go thinking about what we have said and may well be more open to the next Christian they meet.

From Principles to Practice

There are two dimensions to this: the personal and the corporate.

Personal

All of us are called to be witnesses, but we are not all called to do it in the same way. There are a small number of Christians who are very gifted personal evangelists. Their skills are not easily transferable to those of us who have a longing to share our faith but feel that we have little idea of how to go about it. The ideas below are not aimed at the gifted evangelists, but at those who want to learn, but aren't sure how to go about it.

<u>1. Prayer</u>

How do we pray for those who are not yet Christians? The first thing to pray is that God will bless them. Bless them in a way that they will perceive as blessing – meeting their felt needs. If we pray consistently in this way, then not only do we see our prayers answered, but we also find ourselves becoming the answer to our own prayers as God challenges us to be involved in their lives. Secondly we should pray with thanks-giving. Thanksgiving helps us to approach people positively and also inspires us to know enough of what is happening in their lives to be able to offer thanksgiving. Thirdly we should pray for the right opportunity to share faith in words (and the wisdom to recognise the right moment and more importantly the wrong one). We all know the importance of prayer; the reality is that we often neglect this important discipline.

2. Practical demonstrations of Love

This is one of the great strengths of the Methodist Church. Methodist Christians have gained enormous credibility by their engagement as individuals and churches with the needs of their communities. Sadly this has not always been matched by a vision and a longing to help others find Christian faith. In recent history, the church has too often been divided into those who believe in evangelism but don't gain credibility by loving engagement with their neighbours. So their faith sharing is ignored. Others love their neighbours but do not know how to explain the source of the love they are sharing (or do not believe it is appropriate to do so). So the opportunity is lost. Thankfully there has been a growing movement towards holistic mission in recent years. Loving people until they ask why and then speaking of Jesus. This has been embodied in a lot of the youth and young adult forms of emerging church such as Soul Survivor, the Message Trust and 24-7 Prayer.

3. Provocative testimony

An Anglican curate taking up post in her first parish had business cards printed which described her as a 'spiritual consultant'. This has led a lot of people to ask her questions about what she does. Had she put 'curate at St Botolphs', she would have had a lot fewer conversations. How can we describe ourselves and our experiences in a way that elicits questions from our hearers so that they are asking about faith rather than us telling them (whether they like it or not!)? Many faith-sharing courses encourage people to practise telling the story of what God has done in our lives in one minute.[15] If we

15 Lost for Words, CPAS, www.cpas.org.uk; Contagious Christian, Willow Creek, www.willowcreek.org.uk; Blowing Your Cover, www.blowingyourcover.com

can do this, we will often find ourselves in twenty minute conversations about God and faith. Both of these approaches rely on us having the confidence to say something provocative about faith and then not worry about the response. Sometimes people ask questions, sometimes they ignore the opening, sometimes they say nothing at the time but spend time thinking about it later. If we adopt this approach, we generally make it easier for the next Christian who comes along to share too. Another technique much used by Jesus is to answer questions with questions, this again throws the onus back to the enquirer to set the agenda.

The art of asking good questions is a key to effective evangelism!

4. Introductions

Some people naturally have a gift for talking about faith and/or successfully inviting people to evangelistic events or courses. If this is not our particular gift, then it helps if we know who among our friends has this gift and make it a priority to introduce them to our non-Christian friends. If a church runs the Alpha course for some time, research will show who is consistently inviting people to participate. This is a very valuable gift, but because it is quite low-key is often overlooked.

5. Cringe free events

Some churches are better than others at thinking through a progression of events to which people can be invited. In Sowing, Reaping, Keeping[16], Lawrence Singlehurst helpfully points out that most people first encounter church at the simple level of an event that gets across the message that God is good and Christians are okay. Most Methodist Churches have a number of events and activities fulfilling this function (parents & toddler groups; children and youth activities; coffee mornings; social events; community service activities). Some

16 Sowing, Reaping, Keeping, Lawrence Singlehurst, Crossway Books,

of the people who attend such events will be interested in finding out more about the Christian faith if an appropriate activity which meets other needs can be arranged. For instance some of the parents from a parent and toddler group might be interested in attending a Parenting Course which explains Christian principles of parenting. All those who attend will find useful help with parenting skills, but some will be stimulated by the Christian principles underlying the course and will be open to finding out more about faith at an Alpha course or similar. Of those who attend the Alpha course some (but not all) will go on to a full commitment to Christian faith. Most Churches are good at the sowing events, but do not have the sort of quality events which provide obvious next steps to invite people to.

6. Discipling

John Wesley considered that a person responding at a field preaching event was an important moment, but it was in the ongoing life of the Class Meeting that a person was genuinely converted. True conversion was about a life of practical holiness, not just a declaration of the Lordship of Christ. The declaration should be followed by a growing demonstration of that Lordship. That disciplined approach to Christian nurture has been neglected in many parts of the Methodist Church. This has led to a large number of immature Christians who are ill-equipped for living the Christian life and sharing their faith with others. There has been a welcome increase in the numbers of Churches using small groups for discipleship, particularly employing cell church teaching. However it is always difficult to disciple others in ways that we have not been discipled ourselves. The process of raising the expectations of existing Christians concerning the discipling of new converts is an urgent need. Changing mindsets about these deeply held values cannot be done quickly or easily. My own experience of cell church suggests that new Christians find cell values much easier to adopt than those who have been Christians for some time.

How can Churches respond?

There is a wide spectrum of responses. One of the hardest tasks for churches is discerning not only the spiritual needs (and the spirituality) of those outside the church, but also the church's ability to relate to those spiritualities. In the New Testament, we see that Peter was completely convinced of the rightness of the Gentile mission by his experience with Cornelius (Acts 10), however even after that experience, he was personally ill-equipped to respond to that mission opportunity (see Galatians 2:11-14). It was people like Barnabas, Paul, Priscilla & Aquila who had the necessary gifts to engage in the Gentile mission. Peter's role was one step removed from this in gaining permission for the Gentile mission at the Jerusalem Council (Acts 15). All churches can give permission for cross-cultural evangelism (reaching out to the unchurched), but not all of them can actually engage in it. Some churches will decide that they should concentrate on the fringe and the open dechurched.

It may be that in a circuit or in an ecumenical grouping of churches there are enough people to engage in a fresh expression of church that will reach the unchurched. The existing local churches offer support (especially prayer) but have little hands on involvement. Often the best cross-cultural evangelists are those who are fairly recently converted from an unchurched background. It is a challenge to release such people into ministry before they have so assimilated the values of traditional church that they can no longer communicate the Good News to people outside it.

'Equipping your church in a spiritual age'[17], a recently published ecumenical workbook helps churches to look at a whole spectrum of responses to people who are spiritual but not in a traditional Christian way. Each chapter offers pointers

---

17 Equipping your church in a spiritual age, Steve Hollinghurst et al, CTBI, 2005

to how to go about evangelism in a particular context in the light of careful research and highlights approaches which have been pioneered by churches around the country. There are lots of very practical suggestions. The chapter headings illustrate a range of possible responses:

- Rites of passage
- Times and seasons
- Developing the church as the spiritual focus of the community
- Wholeness and healing
- Going out to our communities
- Sacred Britain
- Being with people of alternative spiritualities

Rites of passage
'We want Brooklyn christened but we're not sure which religion yet.' David Beckham

There is still a widely held longing for some sort of spiritual content at key life moments such as birth, coming of age, marriage and death. Increasingly the church can be asked to offer help when life has not gone as well as we had hoped – how do we help people struggling with the pain and guilt of an abortion or marital breakdown and divorce? How can we understand the spiritual longings well enough to communicate faith at these important moments. Sometimes it seems as though those who come to the church have completely different expectations to the church. Instead of a moment that is cherished by both parties, there can be a sense of frustration all round. It's important that preparation for such events involves listening to the 'customers' longings, not just insisting on delivering a doctrinal explanation of the sacrament involved. We also need to think about events that we can offer to encourage people to develop an ongoing relationship with church.

Times and Seasons
Christmas is the obvious opportunity in this category – traditional carols may be the only religious songs known by many people. Christingles are probably the best attended services in the year. There are also lots of opportunities for taking carol services out into the community. Easter, Mothers Day, Rogationtide and Harvest all present good opportunities. Hallowe'en is an opportunity for Christians to stress positive spirituality rather than ghosts and demons (all treats – no tricks[18]). New Year and Remembrance Sunday are also occasions when people are open to spiritual things. There have been lots of creative ways developed to make the most of these opportunities (the Vicar of Dibley's nativity play being a shining example of involving a whole community). These are occasions when a short gospel message well thought out and fitted into a traditional service can help to develop a rhythm of life which draws people into the life of the church.

Developing the church as the spiritual focus of the community
50% or more of the population say that they pray regularly, and 37% of non-church attenders say that they have had their prayers answered.[19]

It should, therefore, be no surprise that English cathedrals are amongst the most visited places in Britain. Lots of other churches are finding that if they open their doors in a way that offers a creative, reflective space, that people will take advantage of it. This sort of approach is often supported more by people outside the church than churchgoers who prefer a 'proper service'. The 24-7 prayer movement has pioneered all sorts of creative ways of praying. Appropriate music and images set the scene. This is particularly helpful at times of national crisis and celebration. The rediscovery of the

---

18 Equipping your church in a spiritual age, Steve Hollinghurst et al, CTBI, 2005, p41
19 ibid p45

medieval labyrinth as an aid to prayer has also struck a chord with spiritual people outside the church. Some churches are more easily adapted to this sort of opportunity than others, but with a little thought, most can help their communities to find time to be with God. A sensitive person coming alongside may then begin a faith-sharing relationship.

Wholeness and healing

A recent survey showed that 39% of the population had tried some kind of complementary or alternative therapy, but only 9% had sought healing prayer from a church.
Soul of Britain BBC 2000[20]

There has been a rise in the number of churches offering a healing ministry. However, these are outnumbered many times over by a range of alternative and complementary medicines, some of which embody Christian principles, whilst others seem to be rooted in the occult. How do we discern which alternative therapies are acceptable for Christians to be involved in and which should not be encouraged? Some churches are also linking healing ministry with physical well-being by setting up gyms and fitness classes – sometimes with Christian meditation as an integral part of the programme. The relationship between healing (or people not being healed) and finding faith is much more complicated than we might like:

We cannot necessarily expect that a miracle in someone's life will lead to belief in the short term. However, in this day and age, in which experience authenticates truth, it can often be the starting point for a spiritual search as the person seeks to understand how he or she has been healed.[21]

Going out to our communities

This is about understanding the various network communities we all participate in and working out how to relate to the

---

20 ibid p55
21 ibid p57

spiritualities of those networks. This may involve a traditional chaplaincy approach or it may involve equipping individuals to demonstrate their spirituality at work, leisure etc. It also encompasses more public demonstrations of faith such as street theatre, evangelism at car boot sales and extreme sports events. Not everyone will be able to be involved in this way and some of our traditional approaches to open air evangelism have only been understood by Christians. It's important to identify people with the right gifts and discern the local culture.

Sacred Britain

There have always been sacred places and sites. Some of them have been 'baptised' from pagan sites, others have been created by various traditions of Christians. These are often recognised by people outside the church. In 'McCarthy's Bar' the lapsed catholic Pete McCarthy travels around Ireland searching for a pint of Guinness in every McCarthy's Bar (of which there are many) but also for the sacred sites and standing stones which abound. He paints a wonderful picture of an agnostic (or possibly atheistic) ex-catholic going on a pilgrimage to a holy island led by a group of monks. Despite his rejection of institutional religion, he still has a yearning for the spiritual.[22] This is shared by many others and the church has responded in all sorts of ways. Traditional places of pilgrimage and worship are ideally placed to attract Christians and non-Christians alike. In more contemporary settings many Christians have discovered that wonderful partnerships can be created in local communities when the church takes environmental projects seriously.[23]

Being with people of alternative spiritualities

Some Christians prefer to stand outside New Age fairs carrying placards denouncing everything that goes on as demonic, others prefer to hire a stall and work with the spiritual seekers trying to help them discover faith in Jesus Christ. The second

---

22 McCarthy's Bar, Pete McCarthy, Sceptre, 2000, pp313-340

23 see www.arocha.org for a good example of this

approach requires a good deal of sensitivity and a willingness to listen and to engage with people in a way that makes sense of their spiritual longings (however uncomfortable those longings may make us). There are several Christian groups who regularly visit mind, body, spirit fairs and other 'new age' events such as the Glastonbury festival (where Ignatian meditation is very popular!). Another area where Christians have become involved is in the interpretation of dreams and the use of Christian prophecy as a proper alternative to fortune-telling.[24]

To the spiritual seekers I became like a spiritual seeker. . . To the New Agers like a New Ager. . . To the Pagans like a Pagan. . . I have become all things to all people that by any means I may win some. *1 Corinthians 9:20-22 (adapted)*

He told them, "The harvest is plentiful, but the workers are few. Ask the Lord of the harvest, therefore, to send out workers into his harvest field." *Luke 10:2*

---

24 Beyond Prediction, John Drane & Ross Clifford, Lion 2001

Bibliography

Evangelising Contemporary Spirituality

Beyond the Fringe: Researching a Spiritual Age, Nick Spencer, Cliff College Publishing, 2005

Evangelism in a Spiritual Age, Steve Croft et al, Church House Publishing, 2005

Equipping Your Church in a Spiritual Age, Steve Hollinghurst et al, Group for Evangelisation, 2005

What sort of Church?

Mission Shaped Church, Graham Cray et al, Church House Publishing, 2004

EmergingChurch.Intro, Michael Moynagh, Monarch, 2004

Useful Websites

www.ciasa.org.uk
www.freshexpressions.org.uk

HEADWAY

A movement of Methodists committed to prayer for revival and witness to the evangelical faith.

The aims of the movement are...

- The promotion of the renewal and revival of the work, worship, and witness of the Church, particularly within Methodism, through prayer and in the power of the Holy Spirit.
- The encouragement of prayer for revival at a personal level, and in the church at home and overseas.
- The furtherance of informed theological discussion in the Church.
- The furtherance of thinking and action on ethical and social issues in a responsible and compassionate way, based on the belief that the righteous will of God must be expressed in the life of society.
- The promotion of joint action with evangelical Christians in all denominations of the Church in local and national events.
- The promotion of mature Christian spirituality in the lives of all members of the Church.

Our basis of faith is that of the Evangelical Alliance, with a specific commitment to the Methodist understanding of salvation, as set out in the 'Four Alls':

- All people need to be saved
- All people can be saved
- All people can know themselves to be saved
- All people can be saved to the uttermost

Membership of HEADWAY is open to any member of the Methodist Church who is in sympathy with the aims and basis of the movement. Associate membership is open to those who are not members of the Methodist Church. Further information from the Membership Secretary:

Mrs Hazel Harwood
1 Linden Avenue, Woodseats
Sheffield S8 0GA